D1443178

The Articles of Confederation

A Primary Source Investigation
into the Document that
Preceded the U.S. Constitution

Kerry P. Callahan

Great American Political Documents

The Articles of Confederation

A Primary Source Investigation
into the Document that
Preceded the U.S. Constitution

Kerry P. Callahan

ROSEN
PRIMARY SOURCE

50164555

Published in 2003 by The Rosen Publishing Group, Inc.
29 East 21st Street, New York, NY 10010

First Edition

Library of Congress Cataloging-in-Publication Data

Callahan, Kerry P.
The Articles of Confederation : a primary source
investigation into the document that preceded the
U.S. Constitution/Kerry P. Callahan.—1st ed.
    p. cm.—(Great American political documents)
Includes bibliographical references and index.
ISBN 0-8239-3799-2 (library binding)
1. United States. Articles of Confederation.
2. Constitutional history—United States. 3. United
States—Politics and government—1775–1783.
I. Title. II. Series.
KF4508 .C35 2003
342.73'029—dc21
                                                    2002010748

Manufactured in the United States of America

On the cover: *The Constitutional Convention*, 1787, by
Allyn Cox, painted in 1974 as a mural for the walls of the
Capitol building in Washington, D.C. The painter has
depicted delegates Alexander Hamilton, James Wilson,
James Madison, and Benjamin Franklin meeting in
Franklin's garden in Philadelphia.

Contents

This drawing of Philadelphia in 1800 portrays the city much as it would have appeared to the delegates to the Constitutional Convention twenty-five years earlier.

Introduction

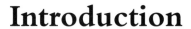

I. The Stile of this Confederacy shall be "The United States of America."

II. Each state retains its sovereignty, freedom, and independence, and every power, jurisdiction, and right, which is not by this Confederation expressly delegated to the United States, in Congress assembled.

III. The said States hereby severally enter into a firm league of friendship with each other, for their common defense, the security of their liberties, and their mutual and general welfare, binding themselves to assist each other, against all force offered to, or attacks made upon them, or any of them, on account of religion, sovereignty, trade, or any other pretense whatever.

—The Articles of Confederation

Drafted on July 12, 1776, America's first constitution, the Articles of Confederation and Perpetual Union, outlined a proposed alliance between thirteen states. Only days earlier on July 4, these former colonies had officially declared their independence from imperial British rule. As governing body of the new nation, the Continental Congress sought to establish a coherent governmental framework that would foster the country's autonomous economic and political survival.

While the Revolutionary War began in 1775, the political movement for independence had developed over a number of years in response to mounting disagreements regarding Britain's jurisdiction in colonial affairs. Prior to the Revolutionary War, relatively few Americans contested the authority of the British Parliament, as Parliament was the legislative branch of the British government that served the king or queen. However, most questioned its ability to represent Americans, and, consequently, its authority to levy taxes in America. "No taxation without representation" was a common colonial protest, even though the concept of taxation by consent was not invented during the Revolutionary era. Understandably, American philosophical and political thought was heavily influenced by British conceptions of natural rights and personal responsibility. Written in thirteenth-century England, the Magna Carta was the first document to address constitutional rights. Embracing the idea of taxation by consent, the Magna Carta declared that "no scutage [a tax paid in lieu of a knight's military service] or aid should be imposed unless by the common counsel of the realm."[1]

Following the lead of the seventeenth-century British philosopher John Locke, many eighteenth-century Americans believed that a republican

In 1215, King John of England, surrounded by his nobles and bishops, signs the Magna Carta, the "Great Charter," a copy of which is shown to the right. The Magna Carta limited the king's authority over his barons and vassals, and is considered one of the earliest English documents protecting the rights of individuals and limiting the power of absolute monarchs.

government gained its authority from the people and that the people or their representatives held the sole authority to tax. All other bodies operated in violation of democratic principles as they exercised arbitrary rule.

It is important to note that the ideals of individual liberty, personal freedom, and participation in the political process hinged on one's place in eighteenth-century America. A narrow understanding of who constituted "the people"—one that excluded black men and women, white women, propertyless white men, and Native Americans—led to a limited application of the rights, privileges, and powers assigned in documents such as the Declaration of Independence and the Articles of Confederation. This is not to say that disenfranchised peoples did not continue to develop their own communities and spheres of influence in spite of restrictions placed upon their individual and collective freedoms. Rather, they acknowledged that the Articles of Confederation was a plan of governance devised by white, propertied men who wielded official legal and political authority within the colonies.

Many colonists were also heavily influenced by a popular political party in Britain, the Whig Party. Whigs adhered, at least in theory, to an idea of personal freedom that centered on the individual. Whigs maintained that the king governed only with the people's consent. Extending this logic, Americans believed that, as they were not represented in Parliament, they had no way of providing their assent to parliamentary regulations. Therefore, any assessment of taxes made by Britain was considered undemocratic.

The British, on the other hand, believed that Parliament represented the colonists through a kind of virtual representation. Parliament did not only speak for its constituents in Britain, but also for imperial interests. It represented the British Empire as a whole. This disagreement over representation fueled America's stance against parliamentary authority over colonial affairs and shaped the governmental structure that would come to be outlined in the Articles of Confederation.

This first constitutional agreement made between the thirteen American states was drafted in July 1776 and officially ratified by March 1787. The final draft consisted of a preamble and thirteen articles. The Articles defined the relative powers of the individual states and the Continental Congress. The framers of the Articles of Confederation created a government based on the sovereignty of thirteen

Four important leaders of the Continental Congress. *From left to right:* John Adams, Gouverneur Morris, Alexander Hamilton, and Thomas Jefferson.

separate states. Representatives from each state met in an assembly called Congress to discuss and promote matters of common concern. Congress acted as the legislative, judicial, and executive body of the government. The Articles of Confederation embodied the traditional view of republican government reflected in the first state constitutions. Like state constitutions, the Articles of Confederation favored the legislative—as opposed to the executive or judiciary—branch of government.

Significantly, the Articles limited centralized national power and instead diffused government power, keeping it localized within state legislatures. Consequently, the states maintained control of the federal government. The Articles also specified that no state could be deprived of territory for the benefit of the country and that all thirteen states had to agree to any amendment of the federal government's power.

A number of issues challenged the effectiveness of the American government under the Articles of Confederation. It could not raise federal revenue through taxes. It had no control over trade, and while it could pass laws, the Confederation Congress could not force the states to comply. As a result, the government was dependent on the willingness of the various states to carry out its measures. Often states refused. Further complicating matters, the Articles were virtually impossible to amend, so unanticipated problems were not easily resolved.

By the late 1780s, the effects of a war-ravaged economy and the political and social uncertainty inherent in the Confederation's transition from colonies to a union of independent states weighed heavily on the Confederation Congress. A number of measures initiated by Congress to respond to problems of national import met with state resistance. Mounting domestic debt and territorial challenges from Britain and Spain, as well as the perceived threat of mass rebellion, led to calls for a stronger central government in the late 1780s. In February 1787, the Constitutional Convention met in Philadelphia to discuss revising the Articles of Confederation. What ultimately developed was an entirely new constitution that created a federal system emphasizing national rather than local or state authority.

The Constitution has served as the ultimate point of political and legal reference in the United States for over two hundred years. In stark contrast, the Articles of Confederation lasted little more than a decade. Nevertheless, a look at the creation and eventual dissolution of the Articles of Confederation will deepen our understanding of the Revolutionary era. As inheritors of a political system in place for two centuries, it might be easy for Americans to think that the present Constitution resulted from a progressive series of neatly ordered historical events. That the Constitution emerged in response to dissatisfaction with the Articles of Confederation, speaks to the complicated and often conflict-ridden way in which the past yields to the present. Perhaps most important, it reveals that history is neither linear nor inevitable, but the result of struggle and compromise.

Chapter One

The Colonies

IV. The better to secure and perpetuate mutual friendship and intercourse among the people of the different States in this Union, the free inhabitants of each of these States, paupers, vagabonds, and fugitives from justice excepted, shall be entitled to all privileges and immunities of free citizens in the several States; and the people of each State shall free ingress and regress to and from any other State, and shall enjoy therein all the privileges of trade and commerce, subject to the same duties, impositions, and restrictions as the inhabitants thereof respectively, provided that such restrictions shall not extend so far as to prevent the removal of property imported into any State, to any other State, of which the owner is an inhabitant; provided also that no imposition, duties or restriction shall be laid by any State, on the property of the United States, or either of them.

—The Articles of Confederation

Modern European imperialism dawned in the fifteenth century, following the discovery of a sea route around Africa's southern coast in 1488 and the discovery of the Americas in 1492. Europe's major sea powers shifted their attention from exploiting lands within the Mediterranean Sea to those across the Atlantic Ocean. England was only one of many European countries interested in the New World and the resources America might yield. In fact, the first European settlement in what is now the United States, the city of St. Augustine in Florida, was founded in 1565 by the Spanish.

The British colonies in the United States developed throughout the seventeenth century. Generally, the growth of the British Empire occurred over a period of centuries and was due in large part to the ongoing competition for resources and markets with their rivals Spain, France, and Holland. During the reign of Queen Elizabeth in the sixteenth century,

The first settlers at Jamestown, Virginia. In 1607 three ships arrived from England with 104 men and boys. Ninety women arrived in 1620 on the appropriately named Bride Ship.

England set up trading companies in Turkey, Russia, and the East Indies, and began the exploration of the coast of North America. Until early in the nineteenth century, the primary purpose of British imperial policies was to facilitate the acquisition of foreign territory. In keeping with mercantile business aims, the British hoped to exploit natural resources and create potential markets for British goods in new and distant lands. In this way, mercantilists endeavored to establish a favorable balance of trade in which Britain's exports exceeded its imports.

Military victories against the Dutch, French, and Spanish in the seventeenth century enabled Britain to acquire most of the east coast of North America. The British established colonies there despite the fact that these lands were already populated by indigenous peoples such as the Abnaki, Mahican, Mohawk, Oneida, Onondaga, Cayuga, Seneca, Mohegan, Nanticoke, Powhatan, Tuscarora, Waccamaw, and Santee.

Over a century and a half after the first British settlement at Jamestown, Virginia, in 1607, the number of British colonies had grown to thirteen—Virginia, Massachusetts, New York, Delaware, New Jersey, Rhode Island, Connecticut, Pennsylvania, Georgia, North Carolina, South Carolina, New

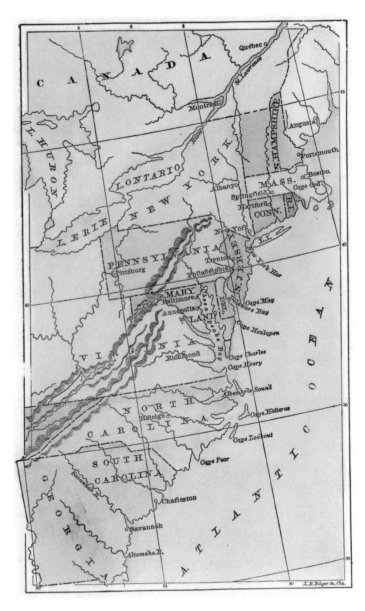

A map of the first thirteen states of the union. After the Revolution, Canada was still a British colony, and French and Indians west of the Allegheny Mountains still prevented rapid westward expansion.

Hampshire, and Maryland. Realizing the economic potential America's natural resources represented, more and more colonists sought to control the region. To that end, they fought not only British rule but eventually asserted their own form of imperial claims on Native American lands. Some Native Americans had a sense of these colonial motives from the start. Powhatan, chief of the Pamunkey tribe in Virginia, remarked to the English leader of the Jamestown settlement, John Smith, that some of his Native American cohorts, ". . . do inform me your coming is not for trade, but to invade my people and possess my country."[1]

As these colonies developed, they did so in the absence of a comprehensive plan. At the outset, all the colonies except Georgia were the result of private financial investment, the projects of merchants and trading companies. The crown granted companies or individual proprietors ownership of a colony along with the power to establish a government and distribute land within that colony. Eight colonies did eventually relinquish or forfeit their charters and became royal provinces.

Established throughout the seventeenth century, these colonies experienced steady population growth and economic diversification. Colonial governments typically consisted of a governor, a council, and a legislative assembly. In colonies that became royal provinces, the governor was appointed by the crown. In Maryland, Pennsylvania, and Delaware, the governor was chosen by the directors of the commercial company managing the colony. Connecticut and Rhode Island were the last of the corporate colonies to be established. They elected their own governors up until the end of the colonial period. While most colonial governors were appointed, the colonial legislators were elected by the citizens of the colony. Property qualifications for voting, as well as the exclusion of blacks and women, limited the number of voters allowed to participate in these elections.

Revolutionary Ideas

During the first century of American colonization Europe was undergoing a scientific revolution. The Polish astronomer Nicolaus Copernicus revealed that the earth revolved around the sun, not the other way around as previously believed. In 1687 the English mathematician Isaac Newton introduced a theory of gravitation and developed a mechanistic theory of how the universe worked. He claimed that the universe functioned in accordance with natural laws that could be grasped by human reason and explained by mathematics.

Concluding that natural laws governed all aspects of existence, many European thinkers projected Newton's ideas into a broad, universal conception of human relations. The power of reason or logical thought, they argued, led to the realization that individuals had a natural right to personal freedom, and that this right should form the foundation of government. In 1690 the English philosopher John Locke published his *Two Treatises of Government*. The ideas he set forth had an enormous impact on Britain and the American colonies.

Effigies Iohannis Locke

John Locke was an English political philosopher who argued against the divine right of kings to rule, and he had a great influence on men like Thomas Paine and Thomas Jefferson.

The first treatise argued against the divine right of kings, a theory that asserted that kings ruled because they were chosen by God, and that these kings were accountable to no one other than God. The second treatise established the social contract theory of government. Believing that people inherently possessed rights to life, liberty, and property, Locke stressed that in order to maintain these rights people came together and agreed to establish governments. Kings or queens were parties to such agreements and were bound by them. When they violated the rights of the people, the people had a right to rebel, overthrow the monarch, and transform their government.

Throughout the eighteenth century, colonial assemblies increased their powers, which sometimes led to conflicts with colonial governors. Significantly, by the early eighteenth century, colonial assemblies voted on taxes and finances and held the power to initiate legislation. Other power struggles unfolded throughout the colonies as well. Many colonists, eager to obtain more land in order to profit from tobacco and rice crops, coveted Native American lands. As a result, during the first half of the seventeenth century a number of major conflicts ensued, such as Connecticut's Pequot War of 1637. The savagery colonial forces

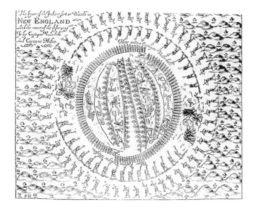

Above, a battle scene from the Pequot War of 1637. Below, a drawing of a Pequot village surrounded and destroyed by colonists. The Massachusetts colonists almost completely wiped out the Pequot tribe.

exhibited in killing and enslaving the Pequots was so staggering, it confounded their Native American allies, the Narragansetts.

Increasingly, native tribes resented the encroachment of colonists on lands where they lived, hunted, and farmed. During the seventeenth and early eighteenth centuries, Native Americans in Virginia and in New England had been subdued by force. Elsewhere, they managed to coexist with the colonists. Toward the middle of the eighteenth century, with the colonial population growing rapidly, pressure to expand colonial territory westward set the stage for further conflict with native tribes. Land agents from the East began appearing in the Ohio River Valley, on the territory of a confederation of tribes called the Covenant Chain, for which the Iroquois were spokespeople. When the British fought the French for North American territory in the Seven Years' War (also known as the French and Indian War, 1754–1783), the Native Americans fought on the side of the French. The French were traders but not occupiers of Native American lands, while the British and British settlers clearly coveted their hunting grounds and living space. Often using religious or racial arguments to justify their avarice, the British colonists employed legal and extralegal means to claim Native American territories.

A seemingly insatiable demand for cheap labor in the colonies also encouraged the flourishing of the slave trade in the eighteenth century. In fact, African slaves were becoming a majority of the population in some colonies. Initially brought to the colonies in 1619 on Dutch slave ships, by the middle of the eighteenth century Africans constituted one-fifth of the entire colonial population. As their numbers grew so did the prospects of a slave rebellion.

Perhaps the most significant power struggle, however, was unfolding between the colonial elites and imperial Britain. Through a series of acts meant to assert royal and parliamentary authority over colonial affairs, the divide between the colonists and the British authorities steadily widened. When England's King George II died in 1760, his grandson George III was crowned king. Along with Parliament, King George III would become the target of colonial ire because of measures such as the Stamp Act of 1765, which imposed taxes on all legal documents such as marriage licenses and newspapers.

To voice their grievances, delegates from nine of the thirteen colonies met in New York City on October 7, 1765. At what would become known as the Stamp Act Congress, the idea of provincial, or colonial, sovereignty gained great momentum. After lengthy debates, delegates to the Stamp Act Congress declared that only colonial legislatures had the authority to tax the American people. A number of colonial assemblies passed similar measures in opposition to the Stamp Act, and these declarations became a permanent feature of colonial law. If the Congress of a national government wanted the power to tax its citizens, it would have to overturn these colonial declarations. Significantly, these laws asserting the authority of the colonies would later impact the distribution of power within the American government during the Revolutionary War and as outlined in the Articles of Confederation.

Chapter Two

The Onset of War

VI. No State, without the consent of the United States in Congress assembled, shall send any embassy to, or receive any embassy from, or enter into any conference, agreement, alliance or treaty with any King, Prince or State; nor shall any person holding any office of profit or trust under the United States, or any of them, accept any present, emolument, office or title of any kind whatever from any King, Prince or foreign State; nor shall the United States in Congress assembled, or any of them, grant any title of nobility.

IX. The United States in Congress assembled, shall have the sole and exclusive right and power of determining on peace and war, except in the cases mentioned in the sixth article—of sending and receiving ambassadors— entering into treaties and alliances, provided that no treaty of commerce shall be made whereby the legislative power of the respective States shall be restrained from imposing such imposts and duties on foreigners, as their own people are subjected to, or from prohibiting the exportation or importation of any species of goods or commodities whatsoever—of establishing rules for deciding in all cases, what captures on land or water shall be legal, and in

what manner prizes taken by land or naval forces in the service of the United States shall be divided or appropriated—of granting letters of marque and reprisal in times of peace—appointing courts for the trial of piracies and felonies committed on the high seas and establishing courts for receiving and determining finally appeals in all cases of captures, provided that no member of Congress shall be appointed a judge of any of the said courts.

—The Articles of Confederation

In 1767, the prominent parliamentary leader Charles Townshend, hoping to strengthen royal control over colonial affairs, convinced Parliament to pass a series of laws imposing new taxes on the colonists. The measures were appropriately called the Townshend Acts. These laws included special taxes on lead, paint, glass, and tea—items routinely imported by the colonists. Further asserting imperial authority, the acts also suspended the New York legislature until it agreed to provide housing for British soldiers.

One of the most important colonial protests in response to the 1767 Townshend Acts was the revival of an agreement to boycott, or not to import, a number of British goods. The non-importation agreement

Charles Townshend, the British chancellor of the exchequer. The Townshend Acts imposed new taxes on goods the colonists needed to import from Britain, and further stimulated the desire for independence.

slowly grew to include merchants in all of the colonies, with the exception of New Hampshire. Within a year, the number of goods imported from Britain dropped almost in half. Then, in response to colonial protests and increasing attacks on colonial officials, Lord Hillsborough, British secretary of state for the colonies, dispatched two regiments (roughly 4,000 troops) to restore order in the city that was becoming a hotbed of colonial dissatisfaction, Boston, Massachusetts. But the daily contact between British soldiers and colonists only aggravated already tense relations.

In fact, armed clashes between British soldiers and colonists in Boston began not long after British troops were introduced. On March 5, 1770, a crowd of sixty Bostonians surrounded British soldiers guarding the

customs house, where taxes were collected and ships cleared for port entry and departure. The crowd began throwing snowballs at the guards. A British soldier was knocked to the ground. When he got up, he started firing into the crowd. Eight colonists were injured and five died in what became known as the Boston Massacre. In light of such incidents, the British government realized that their policies were unsuccessful.

Hours to the Gates of this City many Thousands of our brave Brethren in the Country, deeply affected with our Distresses, and to whom we are greatly obliged on this Occasion—No one knows where this would have ended, and what important Consequences even to the whole British Empire might have followed, which our Moderation & Loyalty upon so trying an Occasion, and our Faith in the Commander's Assurances have happily prevented.

Last Thursday, agreeable to a general Request of the Inhabitants, and by the Consent of Parents and Friends, were carried to their *Grave* in Succession, the Bodies of *Samuel Gray, Samuel Maverick, James Caldwell,* and *Crispus Attucks,* the unhappy Victims who fell in the bloody Massacre of the Monday Evening preceeding !

On this Occasion most of the Shops in Town were shut, all the Bells were ordered to toll a solemn Peal, as were also those in the neighboring Towns of Charlestown Roxbury, &c. The Procession began to move between the Hours of 4 and 5 in the Afternoon ; two of the unfortunate Sufferers, viz., Mess. *James Caldwell* and *Crispus Attucks,* who were Strangers, borne from Faneuil-Hall,

(Above) An inflammatory broadside commemorates four of the five American colonists killed during the Boston Massacre: Samuel Gray, Samuel Maverick, James Caldwell, and Crispus Attucks.

(Facing page) The 1770 Boston Massacre is portrayed by engraver and silversmith Paul Revere. This act of violence pushed Parliament to repeal the Townshend Acts.

Consequently, in 1770, Parliament repealed the Townshend duties on all products but maintained a tax on tea to underscore their authority.

Colonial protests abated temporarily. Then, in 1773, Parliament passed the Tea Act. The new act granted a monopoly on tea trade in the Americas to the East India Tea Company. Incensed by continued British control over trade and monetary matters in the colonies, a group of colonial rebels based in Boston, known as the Sons of Liberty, organized a boycott of East India Tea Company tea. The Sons of Liberty were led by prominent Bostonians such as Samuel Adams, a member of the Massachusetts Assembly from 1765 to 1774. On the evening of December 16, 1773, thousands of Bostonians and farmers from the surrounding countryside packed into the Old South Meeting House to hear Samuel Adams denounce the royal governor, Thomas Hutchinson. Apparently, Hutchinson had denied clearance to vessels that, in deference to the colonial boycott, wished to leave Boston Harbor with tea still on board. Protesters from the meeting headed for the harbor. A group of men disguised as Mohawks boarded three vessels and threw all the tea they carried overboard.

Stunned by the destruction of the tea in Boston Harbor, Parliament quickly passed a series of measures in April 1774 that became known as the Coercive Acts. The colonists referred to the measures as the Intolerable Acts. These acts included the closing of the port of Boston until the East India Tea Company received compensation for the tea dumped into the harbor. Hoping to further assert control over the colonies, the royal governor took control of the Massachusetts government,

THE BOSTONIANS PAYING THE EXCISE-MAN OR TARRING & FEATHERING

(Above left) A British view of colonial protests—American colonists tar and feather a tax collector, while in the background other protesters dump tea into the Boston Harbor. *(Above right)* Some of the stamps affixed to documents printed in the colonies and used to raise more taxes, as mandated by the Stamp Act.

including the power to appoint all officials. Additionally, the British claimed the right to quarter soldiers anywhere in the colonies. Many colonists rallied in support of the rebels in Boston, sending financial and political assistance.

The Continental Congress

With the Townshend taxes, including the one on tea, the stationing of troops, the Boston Massacre, the closing of the port of Boston, and the dissolution of the Massachusetts legislature, colonial rebellion escalated to the point of revolution. In 1774, colonial political leaders set up a Continental Congress—a predecessor to the Confederation Congress. On September 5, 1774, the First Continental Congress gathered in Philadelphia, Pennsylvania. Fifty

(Left) An engraving depicting the first Continental Congress held in Carpenter's Hall, Philadelphia, in 1774. *(Right)* The title page of the published proceedings of that Congress.

members elected by colonial assemblies or conventions represented twelve colonies, all except Georgia. Nine years after the Stamp Act Congress, the First Continental Congress concluded that only the colonies possessed the power to tax the colonies. As there were no colonial representatives in Parliament, the Congress felt that the British had no right to impose taxes on the colonies.

Members of the Continental Congress faced a potential contradiction. While they were not legally bound to the declarations made by the Stamp Act Congress, they did not want to violate colonial law by imposing taxes on the colonists, even in preparation for war with Great Britain. Issuing taxes without popular consent would only threaten the legitimacy of Congress. The delegates passed a resolution, written by the Virginia politician Richard Henry Lee, declaring that "parliamentary taxes on America have been laid, on pretense of defraying the expenses of government . . . in case of war, the colonies are ready to grant supplies for raising any further forces that may be necessary."[1]

The Continental Congress considered both forging a different type of relationship with Britain as well as ways in which they might thwart British control. Finally Congress agreed to stop all trade with Britain and to boycott the East India Tea Company until the Coercive Acts were repealed. But the point of reconciliation seemed to have already passed for many colonial leaders. Through 1774 and 1775, the relatively unorganized Loyalists, those who supported a continued colonial relationship with Britain, were virtually drowned out by cries for independence.

Official Independence

After the first military clash between colonial forces and British troops in 1775 at Lexington and Concord, a meeting of the Second Continental Congress was called in Philadelphia on May 10, 1775. Those present included Samuel Adams, a leader of the Boston rebellion; Patrick Henry, a former storekeeper and Virginia lawyer; and John Adams, a delegate from Massachusetts who would go on to become the second president of the United States. Philadelphia statesmen, philosopher, and scientist Benjamin Franklin, and George Washington, a Virginia planter and retired colonel, also participated.

A number of delegates wanted to declare America independent immediately. Others hoped to avoid a full-scale war with Britain. Congress decided to

Benjamin Franklin

John Adams

Samuel Adams

Patrick Henry

George
Washington

The Second Continental Congress met on May 10, 1775, in Philadelphia. Pictured here are five of its most important delegates, two of whom would later become presidents of the newly formed United States of America.

establish a Continental army and appointed George Washington commander in chief. At the same time, the delegates tried to bring about peace. To that end, John Dickinson, a Philadelphia lawyer who had also been a member of the Stamp Act Congress, drew up a document referred to as the Olive Branch Petition. The petition professed continued loyalty to King George III and urged him to bring an end to the conflict. When the petition reached London, King George III not only refused to look at it, but subsequently ordered the British army in Boston to regard the colonists as enemies.

Further tipping the scales in favor of separation, in January 1776, Thomas Paine, a Philadelphia journalist and radical Whig, anonymously published *Common Sense*. This pamphlet sold more than 100,000 copies in the first three months of circulation and was instrumental in convincing many colonists that the time had come for independence from Britain. At this time, the Second Continental Congress was still in session. They declared a trade embargo against Britain while opening colonial ports to trade with other countries.

Beginning in January 1776, the provincial governments authorized their delegates in Congress to vote in favor of independence. On June 7, 1776, Richard Henry Lee moved that the colonies ought to be free and

Before the delegates to the Continental Congress voted for independence, they sent King George III one last appeal for fair treatment. What came to be known as the Olive Branch Petition was written by lawyer John Dickinson, a member of the Stamp Act Congress. King George refused to read it.

independent states. The Congress then appointed a committee to write the Declaration of Independence. The committee consisted of John Adams; Benjamin Franklin; Roger Sherman, a lawyer from the Connecticut assembly; Robert Livingston, a New York lawyer and politician; and Thomas Jefferson, a lawyer from Virginia. Jefferson, who would go on to become the third president of the United States, was the primary author of the document. The Declaration of Independence was adopted by Congress on July 4, 1776. The Declaration asserted that the colonies were free and independent states, absolved of all allegiance to England. As the Revolutionary War was already underway, the Declaration simply made colonial intentions to separate from Britain official.

In many ways, the Declaration of Independence reflected the influence of John Locke and his social contract theory of government. Jefferson wrote an impassioned defense of popular control over governments and asserted the people's right to rebel and revolt. Again, this conception of the people omitted blacks, women, and Native Americans, illustrating that while the Declaration of Independence is a potent philosophical statement of political rights with tremendous national significance, it is also the product of a certain time, place, and class viewpoint. The

Congress Voting the Declaration of Independence, a circa 1776 engraving by Edward Savage, portrays Thomas Jefferson laying the Declaration on the table at right, while Benjamin Franklin, John Hancock, and other committee members look on.

American Revolution and the documents it produced represented not only a conflict between the colonies and Britain, but also a struggle between those who had access to formal political power and those who did not. This is not to invalidate the political ideals embodied in these documents, but to acknowledge their historic specificity. To a certain extent, though, the Revolutionary movement throughout the colonies was relatively democratic in that it improved the political and economic status of many people.

Included in Richard Henry Lee's motion for independence was a call to develop a plan to confederate

THE PATRIOTIC AMERICAN FARMER.

J—N D K-NS—N, Esq; Barrister at Law.

Who with Attic Eloquence, and Roman Spirit, hath af-
ferted the Liberties of the British Colonies in America.

'Tis nobly done to Stem Taxations Rage,
And raise the Thoughts of a degenerate Age,
For Happiness and joy, from Freedom spring ;
But Life in Bondage is a worthless Thing.

To the left is a painting of John Dickinson by Charles Wilson Peale. At right, Dickinson is depicted in a primitive woodcut from 1772, with his right hand resting on the Magna Carta. Dickinson was the principal author of the Articles of Confederation.

the colonies. As soon as his motion for independence was accepted on July 2, 1776, Congress began working on a constitution that embodied the spirit and principles of the Declaration of Independence. As early as July 12, 1776, a committee headed by John Dickinson produced a draft of the Articles of Confederation and Perpetual Union, unveiling what would become the country's first constitution.

Chapter Three

Adopting the Articles of Confederation

> The United States in Congress assembled shall also have the sole and exclusive right and power of regulating the alloy and value of coin struck by their own authority, or by that of the respective States—fixing the standards of weights and measures throughout the United States—regulating the trade and managing all affairs with the Indians, not members of any of the States, provided that the legislative right of any State within its own limits be not infringed or violated—establishing or regulating post offices from one State to another, throughout all the United States, and exacting such postage on the papers passing through the same as may be requisite to defray the expenses of the said office—appointing all officers of the land forces, in the service of the United States, excepting regimental officers—appointing all the officers of the naval forces, and commissioning all officers whatever in the service of the United States—making rules for the government and regulation of the said land and naval forces, and directing their operations.
>
> —The Articles of Confederation

The framers of the Articles of Confederation recognized the importance of acting as a unified collection of states. No state could carry out war against Great Britain individually nor pay off the debts incurred in such a war on its own. Developing a constitution that would meet the approval of all the states, however, was a daunting task. John Adams once wrote of the Revolution, " . . . the principles of the American Revolution may be said to have been as various as the thirteen states that went through it, and in some sense almost as diversified as the individuals who acted in it."[1] Given these diverse and often competing individual and state interests, disagreements regarding the form the Articles of Confederation should take and the powers assigned therein took some time to iron out. The fundamental question that informed these disputes was whether ultimate political authority should rest in Congress, or with the states. Both conservatives who favored a strong central government and radicals who favored keeping power in the hands of the states hoped to shape the new government in accordance with their ideals.

When the initial draft of the Articles of Confederation was unveiled on July 12, 1776, the document was a long way from ratification. One major source of contention was the question of representation. Should the vote of the states in Congress be in proportion to their population, or should all states share an equal voice in Congress? Actually, the controversy between the large and the small states over representation had developed during the first gathering of the Continental Congress back in 1774. At that point, since population data for each state was unavailable, delegates decided that each colony should have a single vote. This method of voting was maintained during the Second Continental Congress. In keeping with precedent, the draft of the Articles developed by Dickinson assigned each state one vote on all questions before Congress.

When this article came up for discussion on July 31, 1776, the delegates from the heavily populated state of Pennsylvania were the first to object. They were supported by John Adams and Benjamin Franklin, who argued that the small states should only have an equal vote in Congress if they contributed equal financial support to the Confederation. Franklin then submitted a motion in support of voting based on state population.

In response, delegate Samuel Chase of Maryland argued that representation was not only a question of money, but of liberty as well. The smaller states needed to be protected from the power of the larger states. Finally a compromise was reached. The members from the larger states and the conservatives, who wanted to create a powerful central government superior to that of the states, were not able to defeat representatives from the smaller states and the radicals who believed in protecting the autonomy of the individual states. It was decided that each state would have one vote. On certain measures, however, the votes of only nine states would be necessary for passage of an law—specifically, measures dealing with war, privateering, treaties, coinage, finances, and the army and navy.

A second major issue was the basis upon which taxes would be paid by the states into the common treasury. The Dickinson draft stated that the states were to supply funds in proportion to their total number of inhabitants of every age, sex, and status, except for Native Americans. As this count included slaves, the proposal met with determined opposition from states with large slave populations. They demanded that taxation be based on land values. On July 30, 1776, Samuel Chase moved that each state's taxes be assessed in proportion to the number of white inhabitants only. While he admitted that in theory taxation in every state should be according to wealth, it was impossible to assess the value of property in every state.

The taxation debate continued through the summer of 1777. In October of that year, three taxation

Samuel Chase, who later became an associate justice of the United States Supreme Court, was a delegate to the Continental Congress and a signer of the Declaration of Independence.

plans were proposed. In the first, states were to be taxed in proportion to the total population (the original proposal). In the second, taxes were based on the value of lands in each state. In the third, states were taxed according to the value of property in general. After five days of debate, it was moved that taxation be based on the value of all property except household goods and clothing. It was then proposed that taxes be determined according to the estimated value of all lands granted to or surveyed for individuals as well as any improvements made to the land. This motion was carried by a close vote. Each state's contributions to the national treasury would be based on the value of its lands and any associated improvements.

The most intense controversy centered on control of the western lands. A number of states such as Virginia had land claims in their colonial charters that extended beyond their borders to at least the Mississippi River. The boundaries of other states such as Maryland, Pennsylvania, Delaware, New Jersey, Vermont (which had become a state in 1777), New Hampshire, and Rhode Island had finite borders. The "landless" states insisted that the Confederation government be given control of all lands beyond certain boundaries to be set by Congress. The "landed" states refused to cede their territorial claims to Congress and successfully incorporated this view into the final draft of the Articles. But the fight was not over.

Congress adopted the final draft of the Articles of Confederation on November 15, 1777, but it was still subject to unanimous ratification by the states. All states ratified promptly except Maryland, which insisted that the seven states claiming western lands—New York, Massachusetts, Connecticut, Virginia, North Carolina, South Carolina, and Georgia—should cede them to Congress. Maryland did not relent until early in 1781, when Virginia agreed to give up its claims under the old colonial charter that granted rights and privileges to the vast region north of the Ohio River. New York had already given up a claim based on supposed jurisdiction over the Iroquois, and other states eventually gave up their western claims—Massachusetts in 1785, Connecticut in 1786, South Carolina in 1787, North Carolina in 1790, and Georgia not until 1802. Maryland finally agreed to ratify the Articles of Confederation and the constitution became effective in March of 1781.

The Ideal Republic

A product of its times, the Articles of Confederation embodied a type of republican government promoted by eighteenth-century Whigs. For radical Whigs of the eighteenth century, a republic was more than a structure of government based on representation. Whigs believed that monarchs were tyrannical, because they could wield unlimited power. Even popularly elected rulers might ignore the will of the people if given unrestricted authority. Government should not need to resort to force or coercion to maintain control of their citizens. The Articles of Confederation embraced an

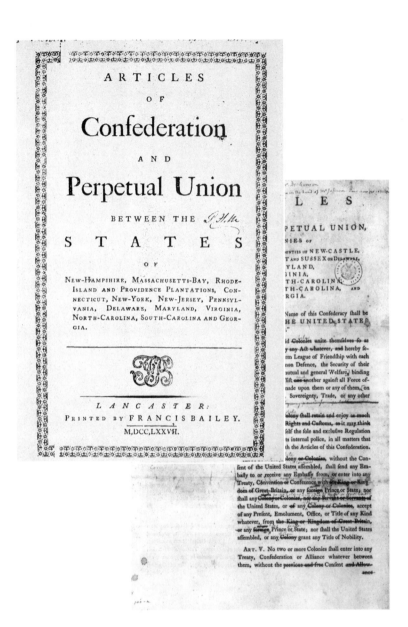

The Articles of Confederation and Perpetual Union, the first constitution of the United States, was drafted principally by John Dickinson. The federal government created by this document was weak, unable to raise taxes or form an army.

50

understanding of government in which virtuous individuals would obey the decisions of state officials and virtuous state officials would work to preserve the Confederation. Conversely, federal officials promoted the general interests of the people and represented their will out of a sense of duty. Because the people were never interested in injuring themselves, there was no conflict between individual liberty and the welfare of the community in the Whig conception of a republic.

Certainly idealistic, the Whig conception of government theoretically resolved the contradiction of forcing people to accept governmental authority in a democracy. People agreed to obey the government as a way of fostering the common good, and in exchange the government safeguarded their individual rights. In a republic all power emanated from the people. As Rhode Island delegates Jonathan Arnold and David Howell wrote to Governor Greene on October 15, 1782: "[T]he weight of Congress rests and bears on the several states; the states bear only on the several counties, in some states, and the counties on the towns. . . in all, on the individuals, the broad basis of power which reared and supports the whole fabric."[2]

In addition, the framers wanted a central government that served the interests of the states and played only a small role in national affairs. A strong central government might enact legislation that threatened the growth of democracy in the states. Further, America was too large, with too many diverse interests, to create a consolidated republic. It would be better to allow the states to carry out republican principles of government and let the central government represent the states.

State Versus Federal Power

Not surprisingly, the Articles of Confederation enabled state governments to retain much power and assigned a subordinate role to the central government. As directed by Article II, "each state retains its sovereignty, freedom, and independence, and every power, jurisdiction, and right which is not by this Confederation expressly delegated to the United States in Congress assembled." In fact, Congress had less power than Parliament had exerted over the colonies prior to the war, particularly as Congress could not regulate interstate or foreign commerce. Certain important acts, in fact, required a special majority. Nine states had to approve measures dealing with war, privateering, treaties, coinage, finances, and the army and navy. Amendments to the articles required unanimous ratification by all the states.

The authors of the Articles of Confederation further protected state sovereignty by requiring members to vote in state delegations rather than allowing them to vote individually. Congress's unicameral legislative assembly was composed of thirteen state delegations with two to seven members from each state. The votes of a majority of delegates from each state acted as that state's single vote. If a state did not obtain a majority among its delegates, the state's vote was counted as an abstention.

A governmental body forged during wartime, Congress focused primarily on military matters during the Revolutionary War from 1775 to 1783. According to the Articles, Congress had the sole power to declare war, determine the conditions of peace, and maintain a navy, while the states maintained militias. When Congress needed troops, it requested a certain number from each state. To guarantee that states shared the expense, the framers decided that Congress could pay all costs out of the federal treasury, including the cost of clothing, equipping, and supplying the Continental army. Congress would then request money from the states to cover these expenses. To that end, Article VIII provided Congress with the authority to requisition funds from the states and required the states to comply. Congress, however, had no means to enforce its requests. Effective implementation of national policies depended on the willingness and the ability of state legislatures to allocate those funds.

Other powers assigned to Congress included the power to negotiate treaties, manage Native American affairs, coin money, manage postal services, and act as judicial authority in specific areas of interstate dispute. Congress also had the authority

This wallet, belonging to an American soldier in the Continental army, contains currency notes printed by banks in different states, which were often not accepted outside those states. Under the Articles of Confederation, the national government had no authority to print money.

to try pirates, to determine appeals in the case of captures, and resolve interstate disputes, if necessary.

Article IX empowered Congress to appoint a president who would preside over its meetings and civil officers who were "necessary for managing the affairs of the United States." The president of Congress supervised its meetings but actually held less power than the delegates. He had no control over the agenda, he could not engage in debate, and he could not vote. The president only facilitated discussion and tabulated votes. Civil officers included a superintendent of finance who oversaw the Confederation's finances, a secretary of war who managed federal troops, and a secretary of foreign affairs who oversaw foreign policy.

In general, Congress maintained the responsibility to make and implement decisions common to all the states. The states maintained the authority to enforce these decisions. The Articles of Confederation protected state sovereignty by making Congress financially dependent on the states. If Congress passed measures against the states, state legislatures had the ability to withhold congressional funds and to prevent Congress from enacting harmful legislation. In keeping with Whig principles, the Articles of Confederation constituted a social contract between the states. It not only acknowledged common state interests, creating a central body that would provide for the national defense and general interests, but also protected state sovereignty by reserving particular powers for the states.

Chapter Four

A League of Friendship

The United States in Congress assembled shall never engage in a war, nor grant letters of marque or reprisal in time of peace, nor enter into any treaties or alliances, nor coin money, nor regulate the value thereof, nor ascertain the sums and expenses necessary for the defense and welfare of the United States, or any of them, nor emit bills, nor borrow money on the credit of the United States, nor appropriate money, nor agree upon the number of vessels of war, to be built or purchased, or the number of land or sea forces to be raised, nor appoint a commander in chief of the army or navy, unless nine States assent to the same: nor shall a question on any other point, except for adjourning from day to day be determined, unless by the votes of the majority of the United States in Congress assembled.

—The Articles of Confederation

Tensions between those who advocated a strong centralized government and proponents of localized power flared as the newly independent nation struggled with an unstable wartime economy, thorny diplomatic issues, and an imperialistic drive to expand westward. When the

A portrait of George Washington by John Vanderlyn, based on a portrait by Gilbert Stuart (1755–1828). Because he painted so many portraits of American patriots, Stuart was called "the father of American portraiture."

Articles of Confederation became effective in March 1781, the presiding Confederation Congress possessed a number of powers—at least on paper. It oversaw foreign affairs and questions of war, resolved disputes between states, and had authority over coinage, the postal service, Indian affairs, and control of the western territories. But it had no concrete power to enforce its resolutions and ordinances because it did not have the power to levy taxes. Congress could only submit requisitions for monies to the state legislatures. There was no guarantee those requests would be honored.

Yet despite these challenges, the Confederation Congress not only survived, but also established important foundations for the future. It concluded the Treaty of Paris in 1783, ending the war against Britain. It created the first executive departments and devised a plan for land distribution and territorial governance in the West.

Initially, there was neither a president nor a prime minister, only the presiding officer of the Congress and its secretary, Charles Thomson, who served continuously from 1774 to 1789. As Congress continued to remain distrustful of executive power, it assigned administrative duties to its committees, heavily burdening busy delegates. For example, over the course of several years, John Adams served on some eighty committees. While the postal department had existed since 1775, the establishment of three new executive departments helped shift some of the administrative burden from the delegates to department administrators. In 1781, Congress began to set up three departments: Foreign Affairs, Finance, and War. Perhaps the most powerful departmental authority was Robert Morris, a prominent Philadelphia merchant with many business connections, who became superintendent of finance.

Morris faced a daunting situation. Throughout the Revolutionary War, in addition to fighting the British, Congress struggled with its own inability to raise resources from the states. Although the states had promised to pay their requisitions, they frequently did not. State leaders often acted according to local rather than national interests. Although Morris was extremely influential, he worked in the service of the Congress and could not act independently of the legislative body. Shortly after the war began in 1776, Congress received little of the money it requested from the states and was unable to fully supply American troops under General Washington's command. Without adequate men, money, and supplies from the states, members of Congress could not

Above, a portrait of Robert Morris, who was in charge of finance for the Continental Congress during the Revolutionary War. Below is a note of credit issued by the Bank of America in 1789.

provide for the Continental army. Determined to make both himself and the Confederation more powerful, Morris devised a plan to create a more financially stable government.

In 1781, as a part of a broad economic scheme, Morris obtained a congressional charter that enabled him to establish the Bank of North America. Morris envisioned that the bank would hold national deposits, lend money to the government, and issue banknotes that would be a stable form of currency. While this was to be a national bank, it was also in part privately owned and was expected to turn a profit for Morris and other business investors. Morris's program ultimately depended on a secure source of government income. In order to raise this income, Morris asked the states to allow Congress to levy a 5 percent tax on imports. A unanimous vote in favor of the amendment was necessary. Rhode Island refused to ratify and prevented the measure from passing.

Frustrated, Morris plotted to dramatically illustrate the Confederation's inability to effectively finance the war and create a stable source of future income. Hoping to capitalize on the Continental army's frustration with the government, in 1783 Morris and his supporters took a dangerous gamble. Washington's army, encamped along the Hudson

River in Newburgh, New York, was struggling against brutal winter weather and fatigue. Their pay was in arrears and they had no guarantee that their promised pay and life pensions for officers would be forthcoming once the war ended.

In January 1783, a delegation of these officers appeared in Philadelphia to present a petition for payment to Congress. Soon they found themselves drawn into a scheme to ally the army and government creditors, the people to whom the government owed money, with Morris and the other nationalists in Congress. They planned to confront the states with the threat of a military coup unless they yielded more power to Congress. The representative to Congress from New York, Alexander Hamilton, was staunchly in favor of centralizing governmental authority. He had served as an aide to General Washington and hoped to entice his former commander to participate in the conspiracy.

Indeed, Washington sympathized with their cause. Washington believed that a military coup was ill-advised, however. When he learned of an unauthorized meeting of military officers to discuss the matter, he confronted the participants. After Washington's moving plea to stay the course, his officers unanimously adopted resolutions denouncing

The disbanding of the Continental army at New Windsor, New York, in 1783 marked the end of the War of Independence. General George Washington said good-bye to his officers in Fraunces Tavern, New York City.

Morris's plan. What became known as the Newburgh Conspiracy abruptly ended.

Congressional attempts to collect taxes from the states and raise revenue were aggravated by an uncertain wartime economy. The country was in the midst of an economic depression, in part the result of war and in part the result of severed trade ties with Britain. Yet, in retrospect, the 1780s were also a crucial period of economic development in America. Battle seldom interrupted farming in New England, and most rural areas benefited from rising prices and wartime demands for food. Output by farmers increased sharply. Released from colonial-era restrictions on trade imposed by the British, rice and tobacco growers profited from an enlarged foreign market for their products. In addition, a growing number of farm households began to produce goods previously imported from Britain.

For a number of Americans, however, signs of economic recovery seemed faint. Shifts in the wartime economy hit merchants much harder. Cut out of the British mercantile or trade system, they had to find new markets. The merchants who benefited most were those who supplied the British or Continental army and those who hoarded goods while demand and prices soared. Throughout the 1780s, new trade agreements opened the Dutch, Swedish, Prussian, and Moroccan markets. Eventually, British trade with America did resume, and American ships were allowed to deliver American products to Britain and return to the United States with British goods. American ships could not carry British goods anywhere else, however. New British trade regulations set forth in the Orders in Council of 1783 prohibited the sale of many American agricultural products in the British West Indies—formerly one of the America's leading markets. All of these changes fed a quick cycle of boom and bust: buying sprees followed by money shortages. This fostered an overall sense of economic instability that lasted several years.

In hindsight, it is difficult to determine if public anxiety resulted from a genuine economic downturn or just from the perception that economic circumstances were grave due to radical political and military changes. Interestingly, one historian has noted that this period of transition "produced bitter complaints in the newspapers and led to extravagant charges against both state and central governments but in no case do the records of imports and exports and ship tonnages bear out the cries of havoc."[1]

Westward Expansion

Like their British counterparts, and in keeping with mercantile and imperial ideology, Congress viewed lands to the west of existing state boundaries and their natural resources as objects that they should acquire. These lands also represented a potential source of government revenue. The Confederation Congress created a precedent-setting policy regarding the development of these areas. Populated by Native Americans, French, and a growing number of American squatters, the region north of the Ohio River had long been the site of overlapping claims by colonies and land speculators.

By 1784, Virginia had ceded all land claims north of the Ohio River, and by 1786 all states had abandoned their claims in the area except for a 120-mile (193-kilometer) strip along Lake Erie, held by Connecticut until 1800. Connecticut called this its "Western Reserve," and retained the land in return for giving up its claims in the Wyoming Valley of Pennsylvania.

As early as 1779, Congress resolved not to treat western lands as colonies. Congressional delegates instead decided that western lands ceded by the states would become separate states, equal in all respects to the existing states. As was the case with the initial settlements along the East Coast, these lands were already inhabited by a number of indigenous peoples. To some extent, the Articles of Confederation acknowledged the adversarial nature of Native American relations in its Article VI. "No state shall engage in any war without the consent of the United States in Congress assembled, unless such State by actually invaded by enemies, or shall have received certain advice of a resolution being formed by a nation of Indians to invade such State, and the danger is so imminent as not to admit of a delay till the United States in Congress assembled can be consulted."

Settlement proceeded at a far more rapid pace during and after the Revolution, despite the Native

Americans' understandable resentment of the encroachment on their grounds. Many Native American land claims were simply ignored. The Treaty of Fort Stanwix (1784) forced the Iroquois to cede land in western New York and Pennsylvania. In the Treaty of Hopewell (1785), the Cherokees lost claims that included lands in South Carolina, western North Carolina, and present-day Kentucky and Tennessee. Also in 1785, the major Ohio tribes lost their claim to most of Ohio, except for land bordering the western part of Lake Erie. The state of Georgia pressured Creeks to cede portions of their lands between 1784 and 1785. In the summer of 1786, secretly supported by Spanish Florida, the Creeks fought to defend their territory. When Spanish aid diminished, however, the Creek chief traveled to New York and, in 1791, negotiated an agreement granting the Creeks favorable trade arrangements with the United States. This settlement, however, did not restore lost lands.

Between 1784 and 1787 congressional policy in the West emerged in three major ordinances. In the Ordinance of 1784, Thomas Jefferson proposed granting self-government to western states as soon as settlers decided to meet and choose their own officials. When the population equaled that of the smallest existing state, the territory would achieve full statehood.

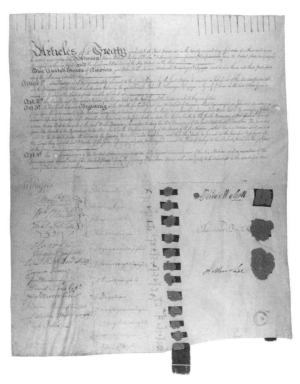

The Treaty of Fort Stanwix, signed in 1784, forced the Iroquois Confederacy to abandon land in western New York and Pennsylvania to the Americans. Many Indian tribes sided with the British during the Revolutionary War, and suffered as a result of the American victory.

In the Land Ordinance of 1785, Congress outlined a plan of land surveys in much of the West. The Northwest was to be divided into townships six miles square along east-west and north-south lines. Each township in turn was cut into thirty-six lots or sections one mile square (640 acres). These 640-acre lots were to be auctioned off for no less than $1 per acre or a minimum of $640 in total. As the plots were too large or too expensive for most farmers, land speculators purchased many of the lots. They hoped to sell them for a profit.

The Northwest Ordinance

In response to land sales and settlements, Congress drafted a new and more specific plan of territorial governance in 1787. This plan modified Jefferson's recommendation in the 1784 ordinance for early self-government. Because Congress feared trouble from squatters who sought free land in these seemingly open territories, Congress endeavored to tighten its legal and political grip on the region. The Northwest Ordinance of 1787 required that each territory serve a period as a colony. Congress would assign a governor, a secretary, and three judges to each new territory. When the population of any territory included five thousand free male adults, it could choose an assembly. Congress would then name a territorial council of five drawn from ten names proposed by the assembly. The presiding governor would still have veto power over the council, as would Congress.

While the assignation of government powers outlined in the Northwest Ordinance resembles the relationship between the American colonists and imperial Britain, there were differences. The Ordinance allowed for statehood when any territory's population reached 60,000. It included a bill of rights guaranteeing religious freedom, representation in proportion to population, trial by jury, and the application of common law. Finally, Article VI of the ordinance permanently prohibited slavery in the Northwest:

> There shall be neither Slavery nor involuntary Servitude in the said territory otherwise than in the punishment of crimes, whereof the party shall have been duly convicted; Provided always, That any person escaping into the same, from whom labor or service is lawfully claimed in any one of the original States, such fugitive may be lawfully reclaimed and conveyed to the person claiming his or her labor or service as aforesaid.

In addition to allowing for the capture and reclamation of fugitive slaves, the prohibition of slavery did not affect slaves already living in the territory. Neither did it stop some slaveholders from bringing slaves into the Indiana and Illinois Territories where there was strong support for slavery.

The Treaty of Paris

As Congress prepared for expansion in the West, they negotiated a peace with their enemy to the East. With the signing of the Treaty of Paris on September 3, 1783, Britain recognized the independence of the United States. The British also agreed to honor a Mississippi River boundary to the West, but as it turned out, Great Britain still kept posts on United States soil after the war. The British justified their continued occupation of the United States by arguing that the American government had not honored the terms of the treaty. More specifically, the United States had not paid its war debts. The peace treaty had committed Congress to recommending that the states place no legal impediment in the way of the collection of the debt, but many states resisted. Many could not support the transfer of desperately needed financial resources to their former enemy. Consequently, the British refused to dispatch an ambassador to the new nation prior to 1791. As early as 1785, however, Congress sent John Adams to London, where he was received by King George III as the American ambassador to England.

In addition to foreign policy troubles with Britain, Spain created political and economic consternation by threatening to cut off American access to the Mississippi. Spanish settlements neighbored the southern boundary of the United States, and the mouth of the Mississippi sat entirely within

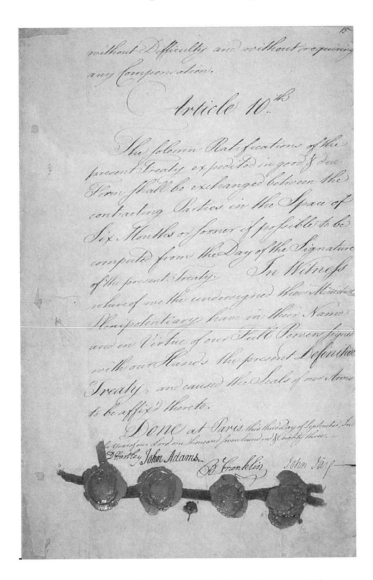

The Treaty of Paris, signed in 1783, formally ended the war between Britain and America and obliged the British to respect American independence.

Spanish Louisiana. Navigation rights to the Mississippi were a matter of great importance because of the growing number of American settlements in Kentucky and Tennessee. In 1784 Louisiana's Spanish governor closed the river to American commerce and forged an alliance with the Creeks, Choctaws, Chickasaws, and other Native Americans of the Southwest against the new settlers.

The potential loss of navigation rights to the Mississippi was only one of many crises confronting

A map of North America showing the thirteen new states of the United States, as settled by the Treaty of Paris in 1783. The British still possessed the territories of Canada, Nova Scotia, and Newfoundland to the north, and the French and Spanish still controlled Louisiana and Florida to the south.

Congress during this period. In spite of the many problems, Congress successfully guided the nation to independence from Britain, negotiated the Treaty of Paris, and developed a long-range plan for imperial expansion in the West. Throughout the 1780s, radical and conservative political forces continued to vie for the hearts and minds of the American public. Their debates raised a question: Was the Confederation a success, having weathered the transitional storms of the Revolution, or was the Confederacy an ineffectual form of government, incapable of responding to the critical domestic and international issues facing the nation?

Chapter Five

A Critical Period

XIII.Every State shall abide by the determination of the United States in Congress assembled, on all questions which by this confederation are submitted to them. And the Articles of this Confederation shall be inviolably observed by every State, and the Union shall be perpetual; nor shall any alteration at any time hereafter be made in any of them; unless such alteration be agreed to in a Congress of the United States, and be afterwards confirmed by the legislatures of every State.

And Whereas it hath pleased the Great Governor of the World to incline the hearts of the legislatures we respectively represent in Congress, to approve of, and to authorize us to ratify the said Articles of Confederation and perpetual Union. Know Ye that we the undersigned delegates, by virtue of the power and authority to us given for that purpose, do by these presents, in the name and in behalf of our respective constituents, fully and entirely ratify and confirm each and every of the said Articles of Confederation and perpetual Union, and all and singular the matters and things therein contained: And we do further solemnly plight and engage the faith of our respective constituents, that they shall abide by the determinations of the United States in

Congress assembled, on all questions, which by the said Confederation are submitted to them. And that the Articles thereof shall be inviolably observed by the States we respectively represent, and that the Union shall be perpetual.

—The Articles of Confederation

In 1787, speaking to graduates at Harvard University, John Adams characterized life under the Articles of Confederation as "this critical period" when the country was "groaning under the intolerable burden of . . . accumulated evils."[1] Indeed, the Confederation was struggling to resolve a number of burdensome issues. Powerful conservatives like Adams argued that the Articles of Confederation aggravated America's problems because they did not allow for a strong central government. Those who supported the Confederation hoped time would smooth out the nation's political, social, and economic rough edges.

Unfortunately, the country continued to grapple with grave foreign policy matters. Spain closed the Mississippi River to American commerce in 1784 and secretly conspired with westerners to acquire the area that would eventually become Kentucky and Tennessee. Britain retained military posts in the Northwest, in violation of the peace treaty ending

the Revolution, and tried to persuade Vermont to become a Canadian province.

Another serious problem confronting Congress was the possibility of government bankruptcy. The nation owed $160 million in war debts and the states rarely sent in more than half of Congress's requisitions. Congress could not force the states to do otherwise. An amendment to give Congress power to levy taxes for twenty-five years, proposed in 1783, met the same fate as previous amendments: it was rejected. In 1784, Robert Morris resigned from his post as superintendent of finance, leaving a congressional committee to handle departmental affairs. The Continental currency was relatively worthless.

Merchants who found themselves excluded from the old channels of imperial trade began to agitate for reprisals. State governments, in response, applied new taxes on British vessels and special tariffs on the goods they brought. State action alone, however, failed to work for lack of uniformity. British ships could be diverted to states whose duties were less restrictive. The states tried to address this problem by taxing British goods that flowed across state lines, but this created the impression that states were commercial rivals. Although these duties seldom affected American goods, business interests lobbied for the establishment of a central power to regulate trade. In 1784, Congress proposed to amend the Articles of Confederation so as to implement uniform navigation acts, but Rhode Island and North Carolina objected. The amendment, like all others, failed ratification.

Mechanics and artisans who were developing small industries sought, and in various degrees obtained from the states, tariffs against rival foreign producers. The country would be on its way to economic independence, they argued, if only the money that came into the country was invested in domestic manufactures instead of being paid out for foreign goods. Nearly all the states gave some preference to American goods, but again the lack of uniformity in their laws put them at cross purposes, and so artisans and mechanics, along with the merchants, were drawn into the movement for a stronger central government.

Shays's Rebellion

In order to cope with heavy state debt, after 1780 the government of Massachusetts levied ever-increasing poll and land taxes. These taxes went mainly to wealthy creditors in Boston. The tax burden fell most heavily on struggling farmers and the poor. Protesting these measures, in late August 1786 a thousand farmers in Northhampton County, Massachusetts, shut down the county court. Frightened state leaders in Boston appealed for public support. Easterners raised funds and sent an army, led by the former Continental army general Benjamin Lincoln to suppress the rebellion. On December 4, 1786, Lincoln expressed his concern for the stability of the nation in a letter to his friend, George Washington:

> The proportion of debtors runs high in this State. Too many of them are against the government. The men of property, and the holders of the public securities are generally abettors of our present constitution, but a few of them have been in the field, and it remains quite problematical whether they will in time fully discover their own interests as they shall be induced thereby to lend for a season out of their property for the security of the remainder. If these classes of men should not turn out on a broad scale with spirit and the insurgents should be in the field & keep it [then] our constitutions [will be] overturned and the federal government broken upon by loping off one branch essential to the well being of the whole. This cannot be submitted to by the United States with impunity. They must send force to our aid, when this shall be collected they will be equal to all purposes.[2]

In Rhode Island, debtors had taken over the legislature and began printing paper money. In New

At top, a woodcut shows Daniel Shays *(left)*, who led a rebellion of indebted farmers in western Massachusetts in 1786. Below, a proclamation by the state of Pennsylvania, signed by Benjamin Franklin, offers a reward for Shays's capture.

Hampshire, several hundred men surrounded the state legislature and demanded that their taxes be returned and paper money issued. The desperate crowd eventually dispersed when state authorities threatened military action.

When the Massachusetts legislature adjourned in 1786 without passing any measure that might help relieve the tax and debt burden carried by some of the states' poorest residents, three counties in western Massachusetts erupted in spontaneous revolt. Armed bands closed the courts hoping to prevent foreclosures. Soon thereafter an armed group under the command of Daniel Shays, a destitute farmer and war veteran, advanced upon the federal arsenal in Springfield, Massachusetts. In January 1787, Shays and his supporters attacked the federal arsenal, but a small militia force scattered the approaching army with a single volley of artillery. Four men died. General Benjamin Lincoln arrived with reinforcements from Boston and subdued the remaining rebels.

The rebels nevertheless achieved a victory of sorts. The Massachusetts legislature omitted direct taxes the following year, lowered court fees, and exempted clothing, household goods, and tools from taxation. An enduring and more significant consequence of the rebellion, however, was the

At left, an address by Massachusetts governor James Bowdoin warning of the dangers of Shays's rebellion. The difficulties experienced by the new national government in raising troops to defeat Shays highlighted the weaknesses of the Articles of Confederation for many people.

political ammunition it provided to forces calling for a stronger national government.

Rumors tended to exaggerate the magnitude of Shays's Rebellion. Those already in favor of creating a stronger central government contended that these rebels were linked to the conniving British and that the rebels threatened the future of the nation. For many the rebellion seemed to foreshadow anarchy. Proponents of Whig philosophy—and there were many in eighteenth-century America—viewed anarchy as the enemy of republican government. Shays's

Rebellion was, some feared, the harbinger of things to come unless the structure of the government was altered. Not all leaders felt this way, though. In response to news of Shays's Rebellion, Thomas Jefferson remarked that "The tree of liberty must be refreshed from time to time with the blood of patriots and tyrants."[3] Nevertheless, Shays's Rebellion fueled the fires for constitutional change.

Calls for a Stronger Central Government

In a letter to former Revolutionary War comrade Henry Knox, George Washington shared his view of Shays's Rebellion and related the sense of urgency some political leaders felt amidst growing fears of political and social upheaval:

> There are combustibles in every State, which a spark might set fire to. In this State, a perfect calm prevails at present, and a prompt disposition to support, and give energy to the federal System is discovered, if the unlucky stirring of the dispute respecting the navigation of the Mississippi does not become a leaven that will ferment, and sour the mind of it . . . We ought not therefore to sleep nor to slumber. Vigilance in watching, and vigour in acting is, in my opinion become indispensably necessary. If the powers are inadequate amend or

alter them, but do not let us sink into the lowest
state of humiliation and contempt, and become a
byword in all the earth.[4]

Political leaders such as Washington, Alexander
Hamilton, and James Madison advocated a stronger
central government and were known as Federalists.
Well before Shays's Rebellion, Federalists had called
for a convention to revise the Articles of Confederation.
Representative Charles Pinckney, a delegate from
South Carolina, had proposed such a convention
in Congress.

In March 1785, commissioners from the states
of Virginia and Maryland met at Washington's
home in Mount Vernon to further discuss issues
related to the navigation of the Potomac and
Chesapeake Bay. Inspired by the successful
negotiation of an interstate agreement, Maryland
suggested a further pact with Pennsylvania and
Delaware in the interest of commerce between
the Chesapeake and the Ohio River. Then, with the
approval of the Virginia legislature, James Madison
invited all thirteen states to send delegates to
Annapolis, Maryland, in order to discuss commercial problems. Nine states named representatives,
but only five appeared at the Annapolis
Convention in September 1786. Maryland, the

New England states, Georgia, and the Carolinas all failed to send representatives. Undaunted, Alexander Hamilton, representing New York, presented a resolution for still another convention to consider all measures necessary "to render the constitution of the Federal Government adequate to the exigencies of the Union."[5]

The Constitutional Convention

The Constitutional Convention finally met in Philadelphia on February 21, 1787, "for the sole and express purpose of revising the Articles of Confederation."[6] The Articles of Confederation espoused the traditional view of republican government, reflected in the first state constitutions, which favored the legislative branch of government. The Articles of Confederation enabled the states, through their legislatures, to effectively control national or federal representatives and federal measures. The delegates to Congress were chosen by the state legislatures and were subject to being recalled. The federal power to raise taxes and armies not only required a vote of nine states but also depended on state monies. The federal government ultimately relied on the will of the states to execute the law.

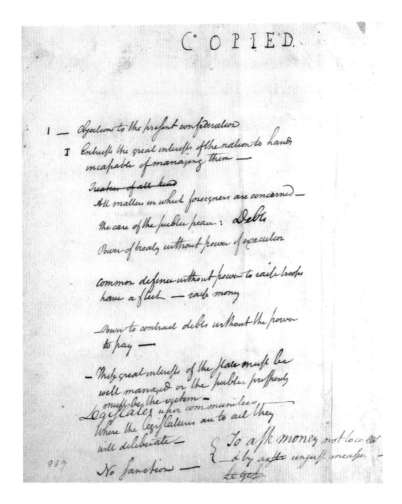

Notes made by Alexander Hamilton in preparation for a speech at the 1787 Constitutional Convention. Hamilton was a Federalist, very much in favor of a strong national government.

In contrast, the constitution proposed by the convention in 1787 provided the basis for a strong national government. Elections to the House of Representatives were by the people directly, not the states, and the federal powers over taxation and the raising of armies were completely independent of the state governments.

Throughout the convention delegates debated what constituted the truest and most effective form of republican government. Those opposed to the Federalist position were known as Antifederalists. Prominent among them were Virginia representatives Patrick Henry and Richard Henry Lee. Lee wrote a comprehensive description of Antifederalism in his *Letters of Federal Fann.* Similarly, Robert Yates, a New York Supreme Court justice, explained the Antifederalist position in his *Essays of Brutus.* Antifederalists proposed adding limited amendments to the Articles of Confederation rather than drafting an entirely new constitution. When it seemed that the creation of a new constitution was unavoidable, they sought to limit the transfer of political power from the states to the national government. They claimed to be the true Republicans and the true Federalists because they understood that republican government was based in small communities where people had ready access to and associations with their government representatives.

The *Letters of Federal Fann* and the *Essays of Brutus* received the attention of prominent Federalists like Alexander Hamilton, James Madison, and John Jay, and the documents prompted them to craft the famous *Federalist Papers,* under the pen name "Publius." In contrast to the radical Whig conception of government that informed the style and substance of the Articles of Confederation, the Federalists believed that, at heart, individuals were self-interested and not necessarily concerned about or motivated to contribute to the common good. They believed that a large republic was not only possible, but preferable to a group of small republics. Federalists felt that individual rights could be better secured through a strong national government if power was divided among different branches. In this way, no one component of the federal system could control or dominate the whole.

The Antifederalists urged that a Bill of Rights protecting the rights of individuals and the states be added to the new Constitution. On September 28, 1787, after four months of deliberation, the convention concluded its business in Philadelphia and forwarded a copy of the proposed Constitution to the states. According to the new plan of government, nine states would have to ratify the Constitution. Many historians agree that had the ratification process followed the procedures outlined in the Articles of Confederation—that amendments to the powers of the government required the unanimous support of the states—it would not have survived.

State conventions gathered from 1787 through 1790 to discuss ratifying the new Constitution. Delaware was the first to ratify on December 7, 1787. On June 21, 1788, New Hampshire cast the ninth and deciding vote. Two of the largest and most influential states, Virginia and New York, had yet to ratify the Constitution. Virginia's convention finally ratified it on June 25, 1788, when it was proposed that the convention should recommend that a Bill of Rights be added to the Constitution. On July 26, 1788, New York ratified the Constitution as well.

Soon thereafter the Confederation Congress prepared for an orderly transfer of power. Congress decided that the new government would be based in New York City. New elections were planned for February 4, 1789. The first meeting of the new Congress would be held on March 4, 1788. On

October 10, 1788, the Confederation Congress concluded its business and the Confederation era came to a close.

Some have argued that the Articles of Confederation failed because they created a weak government dominated by state interests. As a result the Articles could not deal effectively with the inherent demands involved in sustaining a new and growing nation. Others maintain that the Articles of Confederation failed not because they were inadequate, but because the forces that had fostered the creation of a government dedicated to local independence did not support the national government once that independence was achieved. For historian Merrill Jensen, this view was admirably related by Thomas Burke, an Antifederalist from North Carolina who understood Congress as "a general council instituted for the purpose of opposing the usurpations of Great Britain and of conducting a war against her, of forming necessary foreign alliances, directing the army and navy, and making binding treaties." Since this was the nature of Congress and its powers, "all pretence for continuance of a Congress after the war is concluded, or of assuming a power to any other purpose."[7]

Regardless of the cause, the Articles of Confederation are significant precisely because they failed. The government under the Articles of Confederation was the product of the American Revolution, the result of a power struggle between the colonial and British governments. As soon as political leaders recognized the complexities of managing a large nation without a strong central authority, they took the extraordinary step of replacing the government they had so recently formed.

The Articles of Confederation

Nov. 15, 1777

To all to whom these Presents shall come, we the undersigned Delegates of the States affixed to our Names send greeting.

Articles of Confederation and perpetual Union between the states of New Hampshire, Massachusetts-bay, Rhode Island and Providence Plantations, Connecticut, New York, New Jersey, Pennsylvania, Delaware, Maryland, Virginia, North Carolina, South Carolina and Georgia.

I. The Stile of this Confederacy shall be "The United States of America."

II. Each state retains its sovereignty, freedom, and independence, and every power, jurisdiction, and right, which is not by this Confederation expressly delegated to the United States, in Congress assembled.

III. The said States hereby severally enter into a firm league of friendship with each other, for their common defense, the security of their liberties, and their mutual and general welfare, binding themselves to assist each other, against all force offered to, or attacks made upon them, or any of them, on account of religion, sovereignty, trade, or any other pretense whatever.

IV. The better to secure and perpetuate mutual friendship and intercourse among the people of the different States in this Union, the free inhabitants of each of these States, paupers, vagabonds, and fugitives from justice excepted, shall be entitled to all privileges and immunities of free citizens in the several States; and the people of each State shall free ingress and regress to and from any other State, and shall enjoy therein all the privileges of trade and commerce, subject to the same duties, impositions, and restrictions as the inhabitants thereof respectively, provided that such restrictions shall not extend so far as to prevent the removal of property imported into any State, to any other State, of which the owner is an inhabitant; provided also that no imposition, duties or restriction shall be laid by any State, on the property of the United States, or either of them.

If any person guilty of, or charged with, treason, felony, or other high misdemeanor in any State, shall flee from justice, and be found in any of the United States, he shall, upon demand of the Governor or executive power of the State from which he fled, be delivered up and removed to the State having jurisdiction of his offense.

Full faith and credit shall be given in each of these States to the records, acts, and judicial proceedings of the courts and magistrates of every other State.

V. For the most convenient management of the general interests of the United States, delegates shall be annually appointed in such manner as the legislatures of each State shall direct, to meet in Congress on the first Monday in November, in every year, with a power reserved to each State to recall its delegates, or any of them, at any time within the year, and to send others in their stead for the remainder of the year.

No State shall be represented in Congress by less than two, nor more than seven members; and no person shall be capable of being a delegate for more than three years in any term of six years; nor shall any person, being a delegate, be capable of holding any office under the United States, for which he, or another for his benefit, receives any salary, fees or emolument of any kind.

Each State shall maintain its own delegates in a meeting of the States, and while they act as members of the committee of the States.

In determining questions in the United States in Congress assembled, each State shall have one vote.

Freedom of speech and debate in Congress shall not be impeached or questioned in any court or place out of Congress, and the members of Congress shall be protected in their persons from arrests or imprisonments, during the time of their going to and from, and attendance on Congress, except for treason, felony, or breach of the peace.

VI. No State, without the consent of the United States in Congress assembled, shall send any embassy to, or receive any embassy from, or enter into any conference, agreement, alliance or treaty with any King, Prince or State; nor shall any person holding any office of profit or trust under the United States, or any of them, accept any present, emolument, office or title of any kind whatever from any King, Prince or foreign State; nor shall the United States in Congress assembled, or any of them, grant any title of nobility.

No two or more States shall enter into any treaty, confederation or alliance whatever between them, without the consent of the United States in Congress assembled, specifying accurately the purposes for which the same is to be entered into, and how long it shall continue.

No State shall lay any imposts or duties, which may interfere with any stipulations in treaties, entered into by the United States in Congress assembled, with any King, Prince or State, in pursuance of any treaties already proposed by Congress, to the courts of France and Spain.

No vessel of war shall be kept up in time of peace by any State, except such number only, as shall be deemed necessary by the United States in Congress assembled, for the defense of such State, or its trade; nor shall any body of forces be kept up by any State in time of peace, except such number only, as in the judgement of the United States in Congress assembled, shall be deemed requisite to garrison the forts necessary for the defense of such State; but every State shall always keep up a well-regulated and disciplined militia, sufficiently armed and accoutered, and shall provide and constantly have ready for use, in public stores, a due number of filed pieces and tents, and a proper quantity of arms, ammunition and camp equipage.

No State shall engage in any war without the consent of the United States in Congress assembled, unless such State be actually invaded by enemies, or shall have received certain advice of a resolution being formed by some nation of Indians to invade such State, and the danger is so imminent as not to admit of a delay till the United States in Congress assembled can be consulted; nor shall any State grant commissions to any ships or vessels of war, nor letters of marque or reprisal, except it be after a declaration of war by the United States in Congress assembled, and then only against the Kingdom or State and the subjects thereof, against which war has been so declared, and under such regulations as shall be established by the United States in Congress assembled, unless such State be infested by pirates, in which case vessels of war may be fitted out for that occasion, and kept so long as the danger shall continue, or until the United States in Congress assembled shall determine otherwise.

VII. When land forces are raised by any State for the common defense, all officers of or under the rank of colonel, shall be appointed by the legislature of each State respectively, by whom such forces shall be raised, or in such manner as such State shall direct, and all vacancies shall be filled up by the State which first made the appointment.

VIII. All charges of war, and all other expenses that shall be incurred for the common defense or general welfare, and allowed by the United States in Congress assembled, shall be defrayed out of a common treasury, which shall be supplied by the several

States in proportion to the value of all land within each State, granted or surveyed for any person, as such land and the buildings and improvements thereon shall be estimated according to such mode as the United States in Congress assembled, shall from time to time direct and appoint.

The taxes for paying that proportion shall be laid and levied by the authority and direction of the legislatures of the several States within the time agreed upon by the United States in Congress assembled.

IX. The United States in Congress assembled, shall have the sole and exclusive right and power of determining on peace and war, except in the cases mentioned in the sixth article—of sending and receiving ambassadors—entering into treaties and alliances, provided that no treaty of commerce shall be made whereby the legislative power of the respective States shall be restrained from imposing such imposts and duties on foreigners, as their own people are subjected to, or from prohibiting the exportation or importation of any species of goods or commodities whatsoever—of establishing rules for deciding in all cases, what captures on land or water shall be legal, and in what manner prizes taken by land or naval forces in the service of the United States shall be divided or appropriated—of granting letters of marque and reprisal in times of peace—appointing courts for the trial of piracies and felonies committed on the high seas and establishing courts for receiving and determining finally appeals in all cases of captures, provided that no member of Congress shall be appointed a judge of any of the said courts.

The United States in Congress assembled shall also be the last resort on appeal in all disputes and differences now subsisting or that hereafter may arise between two or more States concerning boundary, jurisdiction or any other causes whatever; which authority shall always be exercised in the manner following. Whenever the legislative or executive authority or lawful agent of any State in controversy with another shall present a petition to Congress stating the matter in question and praying for a hearing, notice thereof shall be given by order of Congress to the legislative or executive authority of the other State in controversy, and a day assigned for the appearance of the parties by their lawful agents, who shall then be directed to appoint by joint consent, commissioners or judges to constitute a court for hearing and determining the matter in question: but if they cannot agree, Congress shall name three persons out of each of the United States, and from the list of such persons each party shall alternately strike out one, the petitioners beginning, until the number shall be reduced to thirteen; and from that number not less than seven, nor more than nine names as Congress shall direct, shall in the presence of Congress be drawn out by lot, and the persons whose names shall be so drawn or any five of them, shall be commissioners or judges, to hear and finally determine the controversy, so always as a major part of the judges who shall hear the cause shall agree in the determination: and if either party shall neglect to attend at the day appointed, without showing reasons, which Congress shall judge sufficient, or being present shall refuse to strike, the Congress shall proceed to nominate three persons out of each State, and the secretary of Congress shall strike in behalf of such party absent or refusing; and the judgement and sentence of the court to be appointed, in the manner before prescribed, shall be final and conclusive; and if any of the parties shall refuse to submit to the authority of such court, or to appear or defend their claim or cause, the court shall nevertheless proceed to pronounce sentence, or judgement, which shall in like manner be final and decisive, the judgement or sentence and other proceedings being in either case transmitted to Congress, and lodged among the acts of Congress for the security of the parties concerned: provided that every commissioner, before he sits in judgement, shall take an oath to be administered by one of the judges of the supreme or superior court of the State, where the cause shall be tried, 'well and truly to hear and determine the matter in question, according to the best of his judgement, without favor, affection or hope of reward': provided also, that no State shall be deprived of territory for the benefit of the United States.

All controversies concerning the private right of soil claimed under different grants of two or more States, whose jurisdictions as they may respect such lands, and the States which passed such grants are adjusted, the said grants or either of them being at the same time claimed to have originated antecedent to such settlement of jurisdiction, shall on the petition of either party to the Congress of the United States, be finally determined as near as may be in the same manner as is before prescribed for deciding disputes respecting territorial jurisdiction between different States.

The United States in Congress assembled shall also have the sole and exclusive right and power of regulating the alloy and value of coin struck by their own authority, or by that of the respective States—fixing the standards of weights and measures throughout the United States—regulating the trade and managing all affairs with the Indians, not members of any of the States, provided that the legislative right of any State within its own limits be not infringed or violated—establishing or regulating post offices from one State to another, throughout all the United States, and exacting such postage on the papers passing through the same as may be requisite to defray the expenses of the said office—appointing all officers of the land forces, in the service of the United States, excepting regimental officers—appointing all the officers of the naval forces, and commissioning all officers whatever in the service of the United States—making rules for the government and regulation of the said land and naval forces, and directing their operations.

The United States in Congress assembled shall have authority to appoint a committee, to sit in the recess of Congress, to be denominated 'A Committee of the States', and to consist of one delegate from each State; and to appoint such other committees and civil officers as may be necessary for managing the general affairs of the United States under their direction;

—to appoint one of their members to preside, provided that no person be allowed to serve in the office of president more than one year in any term of three years; to ascertain the necessary sums of money to be raised for the service of the United States, and to appropriate and apply the same for defraying the public expenses—to borrow money, or emit bills on the credit of the United States, transmitting every half-year to the respective States an account of the sums of money so borrowed or emitted;

—to build and equip a navy—to agree upon the number of land forces, and to make requisitions from each State for its quota, in proportion to the number of white inhabitants in such State; which requisition shall be binding, and thereupon the legislature of each State shall appoint the regimental officers, raise the men and cloath, arm and equip them in a solid-like manner, at the expense of the United States; and the officers and men so cloathed, armed and equipped shall march to the place appointed, and within the time agreed on by the United States in Congress assembled. But if the United States in Congress assembled shall, on consideration of circumstances judge proper that any State should not raise men, or should raise a smaller number of men than the quota thereof, such extra number shall be raised, officered, cloathed, armed and equipped in the same manner as the quota of each State, unless the legislature of such State shall judge that such extra number cannot be safely spread out in the same, in which case they shall raise, officer, cloath, arm, and equip as many of such extra number as they judge can be safely spared. And the officers and men so cloathed, armed, and equipped, shall march to the place appointed, and within the time agreed on by the United States in Congress assembled.

The United States in Congress assembled shall never engage in a war, nor grant letters of marque or reprisal in time of peace, nor enter into any treaties or alliances, nor coin money, nor regulate the value thereof, nor ascertain the sums and expenses necessary for the defense and welfare of the United States, or any of them, nor emit bills, nor borrow money on the credit of the United States, nor appropriate money, nor agree upon the number of vessels of war, to be built or purchased, or the number of land or sea forces to be raised, nor appoint a commander in chief of the army or navy, unless nine States assent to the same: nor shall a question on any other point, except for adjourning from day to day be determined, unless by the votes of the majority of the United States in Congress assembled.

The Congress of the United States shall have power to adjourn to any time within the year, and to any place within the United States, so that no period of adjournment be for a longer duration than the space of six months, and shall publish the journal of their proceedings monthly, except such parts thereof relating to treaties, alliances or military operations, as in their judgement require secrecy; and the yeas and nays of the delegates of each State on any question shall be entered on the journal, when it is desired by any delegates of a State, or any of them, at his or their request shall be furnished with a transcript of the said journal, except such parts as are above excepted, to lay before the legislatures of the several States.

X. The Committee of the States, or any nine of them, shall be authorized to execute, in the recess of Congress, such of the powers of Congress as the United States in Congress assembled, by the consent of the nine States, shall from time to time think expedient to vest them with; provided that no power be delegated to the said Committee, for the exercise of which, by the Articles of Confederation, the voice of nine States in the Congress of the United States assembled be requisite.

XI. Canada acceding to this confederation, and adjoining in the measures of the United States, shall be admitted into, and entitled to all the advantages of this Union; but no other colony shall be admitted into the same, unless such admission be agreed to by nine States.

XII. All bills of credit emitted, monies borrowed, and debts contracted by, or under the authority of Congress, before the assembling of the United States, in pursuance of the present confederation, shall be deemed and considered as a charge against the United States, for payment and satisfaction whereof the said United States, and the public faith are hereby solemnly pledged.

XIII. Every State shall abide by the determination of the United States in Congress assembled, on all questions which by this confederation are submitted to them. And the Articles of this Confederation shall be inviolably observed by every State, and the Union shall be perpetual; nor shall any alteration at any time hereafter be made in any of them; unless such alteration be agreed to in a Congress of the United States, and be afterwards confirmed by the legislatures of every State.

And Whereas it hath pleased the Great Governor of the World to incline the hearts of the legislatures we respectively represent in Congress, to approve of, and to authorize us to ratify the said Articles of Confederation and perpetual Union. Know Ye that we the undersigned delegates, by virtue of the power and authority to us given for that purpose, do by these presents, in the name and in behalf of our respective constituents, fully and entirely ratify and confirm each and every of the said Articles of

Confederation and perpetual Union, and all and singular the matters and things therein contained: And we do further solemnly plight and engage the faith of our respective constituents, that they shall abide by the determinations of the United States in Congress assembled, on all questions, which by the said Confederation are submitted to them. And that the Articles thereof shall be inviolably observed by the States we respectively represent, and that the Union shall be perpetual.

In Witness whereof we have hereunto set our hands in Congress. Done at Philadelphia in the State of Pennsylvania the ninth day of July in the Year of our Lord One Thousand Seven Hundred and Seventy-Eight, and in the Third Year of the independence of America.

On the part and behalf of the State of New Hampshire:

Josiah Bartlett
John Wentworth Junr.
August 8th 1778

On the part and behalf of The State of Massachusetts Bay:

John Hancock
Francis Dana
Samuel Adams

James Lovell
Elbridge Gerry
Samuel Holten

On the part and behalf of the State of Rhode Island and Providence Plantations:

William Ellery
John Collins
Henry Marchant

On the part and behalf of the State of Connecticut:

Roger Sherman
Titus Hosmer
Samuel Huntington
Andrew Adams
Oliver Wolcott

On the Part and Behalf of the State of New York:

James Duane
Wm Duer
Francis Lewis
Gouv Morris

On the Part and in Behalf of the State of New Jersey, November 26, 1778.

Jno Witherspoon
Nathaniel Scudder

On the part and behalf of the State of Pennsylvania:

Robt Morris
William Clingan
Daniel Roberdeau
Joseph Reed
John Bayard Smith
22nd July 1778

On the part and behalf of the State of Delaware:

Tho Mckean February 12, 1779
John Dickinson May 5th 1779
Nicholas Van Dyke

On the part and behalf of the State of Maryland:

John Hanson March 1 1781
Daniel Carroll Do

On the Part and Behalf of the State of Virginia:

Richard Henry Lee
Jno Harvie
John Banister
Francis Lightfoot Lee
Thomas Adams

On the part and Behalf of the State of No Carolina:

John Penn July 21St 1778
Corns Harnett
Jno Williams

On the part and behalf of the State of South Carolina:

Henry Laurens
Richd Hutson
William Henry Drayton
Thos Heyward Junr
Jno Mathews

On the part and behalf of the State of Georgia:

Jno Walton 24th July 1778
Edwd Telfair
Edwd Langworthy

Agreed to by Congress 15 November 1777
In force after ratification by Maryland, 1 March 1781

Glossary

abstention   The act of withholding one's vote or opinion, either for or against a position.

arrears   The state of being behind in the discharge of obligations.

autonomy   The quality or state of being self-governing.

class   A group sharing the same economic or social status.

congress   A formal meeting of delegates for discussion and usually action on some question.

exploit   To make use of something or someone meanly or unjustly for one's own advantage.

foreclosure   To foreclose or preclude a mortgage.

ordinance   An authoritative decree, direction, or order; a law set forth by governmental authority.

parliament   A formal conference for the discussion of public affairs; specifically, an assemblage of the nobility, clergy, and commons called together by the British sovereign as the supreme legislative body in the United Kingdom.

poll tax   A tax of a fixed amount per person levied on adults.

privateer   An armed private ship licensed to attack enemy shipping.

requisition   A demand or request usually made with authority; a written request for something authorized but not made available automatically.

sovereignty   Supreme power, especially over a body politic; freedom from external control or controlling influence.

squatter   One that settles on property without right or title or payment of rent.

tariff   A schedule of fees imposed by a government on imported or, in some countries, exported goods.

unicameral   Having or consisting of one legislative chamber.

veto   The power of one branch of government to prohibit or forbid the carrying out of projects attempted by another department.

For More Information

American Historical Association
400 A Street SE
Washington, DC 20003-3889
(202) 544-2422
Web site: http://www.theaha.org

American Independence Museum
One Governor's Lane
Exeter, NH 03833
(603) 772-2622
Web site: http://www.independencemuseum.org

Bunker Hill Pavilion
55 Constitution Road
Charlestown, MA 02129
(617) 241-7575

The Library of Congress
101 Independence Avenue SE
Washington, DC 20540
(202) 707-5000
Web site: http://www.loc.gov

National Constitution Center
The Bourse, Suite 560, 111 S. Independence Mall E.
Philadelphia, PA 19106
(215) 923-0004
Web site: http://www.constitutioncenter.org/

National Museum of American History
14th Street and Constitution Avenue NW
Washington, DC 20560
(202) 357-1784
Web site: http://americanhistory.si.edu/

Smithsonian Institution
P.O. Box 37012
SI Building, Room 153
Washington, DC 20013-7012
(202) 357-2020
Web site: http://www.smithsonian.org

Web Sites

Due to the changing nature of Internet links, the
Rosen Publishing Group, Inc., has developed an
online list of Web sites related to the subject of this
book. This site is updated regularly. Please use this
link to access the list:

http://www.rosenlinks.com/gapd/arco

For Further Reading

Feinberg, Barbara Silberdick. *The Articles of Confederation: The First Constitution of the United States*. Brookfield, CT: Twenty-First Century Books, 2002.

Hart, Albert Bushnell. *Proposals to Amend the Articles of Confederation, 1781–1789*. New York: A. Lovell & Company, 1896.

Hoffert, Robert W. *A Politics of Tensions: The Articles of Confederation and American Political Ideas*. Niwot, CO: University Press of Colorado, 1992.

Hull, Mary. *Shays' Rebellion and the Constitution in American History*. Berkeley Heights, NJ: Enslow Publishers, Inc., 2000.

Hull, William Isaac. *Maryland, Independence, and the Confederation*. Baltimore: J. Murphy & Company, 1891.

Ketchum, Ralph, ed. *The Anti-Federalist Papers and the Constitutional Convention Debates*. New York: New American Library, 1986.

Tindall, George Brown. *America: A Narrative History*. New York: W.W. Norton and Company, 1988.

Wood, Gordon S. *The Creation of the American Republic*. New York: W.W. Norton and Company, 1972.

Bibliography

Bailyn, Bernard. *The Ideological Origins of the American Revolution.* Cambridge, MA: Belknap Press of Harvard University Press, 1967.

Colbert, David, ed. *Eyewitness to America: 500 years of America in the Words of Those Who Saw It Happen.* New York: Pantheon Books, 1997.

Davis, David Brion, and Steven Mintz. *The Boisterous Sea of Liberty: A Documentary History of America from Discovery through the Civil War.* New York: Oxford University Press, 1998.

Dougherty, Keith L. *Collective Action under the Articles of Confederation.* New York: Cambridge University Press, 2001.

Dry, Murray. "The Constitutional Thought of the Anti-Federalists." Reprinted from *The Constitution: A Bicentennial Chronicle*, Fall 1985. Published by Project '87 of the American Political Science Association and the American Historical Association.

Fiske, John. *The Critical Period of American History, 1783–1789.* Boston: Houghton Mifflin Company, 1916.

Jensen, Merrill. *The Articles of Confederation: An Interpretation of the Social-Constitutional History of the American Revolution, 1774–1781.* Madison, WI: University of Wisconsin Press, 1940.

Yarborough, Jean. "The Federalist." Reprinted from *The Constitution: A Bicentennial Chronicle,* Fall 1985. Published by Project '87 of the American Political Science Association and the American Historical Association.

Zinn, Howard. *A People's History of the United States: 1492–Present.* New York: Harper Collins, 1980.

Source Notes

Introduction

1. Keith L. Dougherty, *Collective Action under the Articles of Confederation* (New York: Cambridge University Press, 2001), p. 21.

Chapter One

1. George Brown Tindall, *America: A Narrative History, Volume One* (New York: W. W. Norton & Company, 1988), p. 154.

Chapter Two

1. Keith L. Dougherty, *Collective Action under the Articles of Confederation* (New York: Cambridge University Press, 2001), p. 22.

Chapter Three

1. John Adams to Mercy Warren Quincy, July 20, 1807, from the *Massachusetts Historical Collections*, 5th series, 4: 338 (Boston, 1878).
2. Jonathan Arnold and David Howell to Governor Greene, October 15, 1782, from Patrick T. Conley, *First in War, Last in Peace: Rhode Island*

and the Constitution (Providence, RI: Rhode Island Publications Society, 1987), p. 46.

Chapter Four

1. George Brown Tindall, *America: A Narrative History, Volume One* (New York: W. W. Norton & Company, 1988), p. 272.

Chapter Five

1. George Brown Tindall, *America: A Narrative History, Volume One* (New York: W. W. Norton & Company, 1988), p. 265
2. David Brion Davis and Steven Mintz, *The Boisterous Sea of Liberty: A Documentary History of America from Discovery through the Civil War* (New York: Oxford University Press, 1998), p.229.
3. Tindall, p. 278
4. Davis and Mintz, p. 231
5. Tindall, p. 279
6. Ibid.
7. Merrill Jensen, *The Articles of Confederation: An Interpretation of the Social-Constitutional History of the American Revolution, 1774–1781* (Madison, WI: University of Wisconsin Press, 1940), p. 244.

Primary Source Image List

Index

124

About the Author

Kerry P. Callahan is an editor and freelance writer living in the Rocky Mountain West.

Credits

Cover, p. 58 Architect of the Capitol; pp. 6, 37 (top left and right, middle right, bottom), 42 (left), 61 (top) Independence National Historical Park; pp. 9 (top), 23 (top), 29, 31, 34, 39 (inset), 50, 54, 61 (bottom), 64 © Hulton/Archive/Getty Images; p. 9 (bottom) Perot Foundation, courtesy of the National Archives and Records Administration; pp. 12, 30, 37 (middle left) 41, 47, 81(bottom) Library of Congress, Prints and Photographs Division; pp. 16, 18, 33 (right) © Bettmann/Corbis; p. 21 © Archivo Iconografico, S.A./Corbis; pp. 23 (bottom), 42 (right), 83 Library of Congress, Rare Book and Special Collections Division; p. 33 (left) © Corbis; pp. 39, 87 Library of Congress, Manuscript Division; pp. 69, 73 Old Military and Civil Records, National Archives and Records Administration; p. 74 Library of Congress, Geography and Map Division; p. 81(top) National Portrait Gallery, Smithsonian Institution/Art Resource, NY.

Editor

Jake Goldberg

Design and Layout

Les Kanturek